W9-COV-461

BMX RACING

BY JACK DAVID

BELLWETHER MEDIA • MINNEAPOLIS, MN

TORQUE

Are you ready to take it to the extreme?
Torque books thrust you into the action-packed world
of sports, vehicles, and adventure. These books may
include dirt, smoke, fire, and dangerous stunts.
WARNING: read at your own risk.

This edition first published in 2008 by Bellwether Media.

No part of this publication may be reproduced in whole or in part without written
permission of the publisher. For information regarding permission, write to Bellwether
Media Inc., Attention: Permissions Department, Post Office Box 1C, Minnetonka, MN
55345-9998.

Library of Congress Cataloging-in-Publication Data
David, Jack, 1968-
  BMX racing / by Jack David.
    p. cm. -- (Torque : action sports)
  Summary: "Photographs of amazing feats accompany engaging information about
BMX racing. The combination of high-interest subject matter and light text is intended to
engage readers in grades 3 through 7"--Provided by publisher.
  Includes bibliographical references and index.
  ISBN-13: 978-1-60014-122-5 (hardcover : alk. paper)
  ISBN-10: 1-60014-122-6 (hardcover : alk. paper)
  1. Bicycle motocross--Juvenile literature. I. Title.

  GV1049.3.D38 2008
  796.6'2--dc22   2007016792

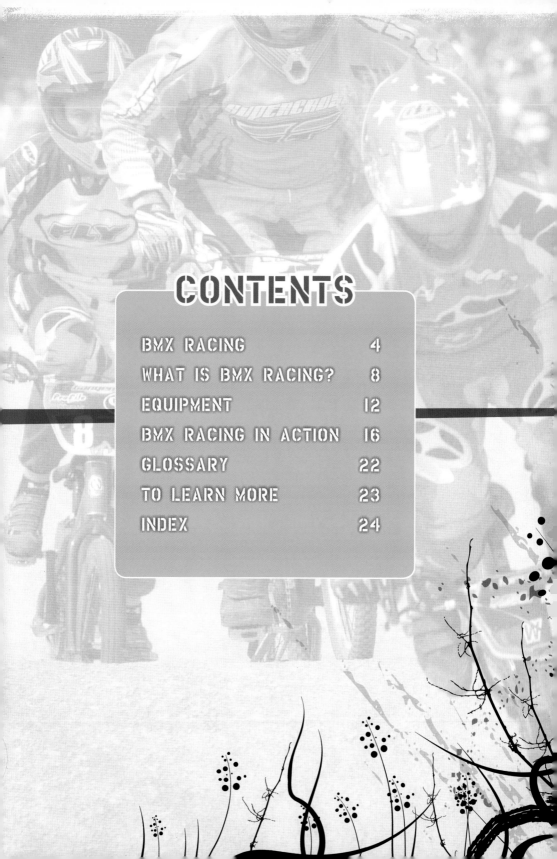

CONTENTS

BMX RACING

A BMX racer pushes down hard on his pedals. He is leading the final lap of the race. A big group of riders is right behind him. He can hear them getting closer.

He tries to stay in front. His bike launches smoothly over a jump. The rear tire kicks up dirt as it skids around a turn. His foot slips off the pedal.

The mistake slows the bike. It doesn't hit the next jump with enough speed. Two other riders fly past. He's lost the lead. He keeps pedaling because he still has a chance to win.

WHAT IS BMX RACING?

Bicycle motocross (BMX) racing grew out of the sport of **motocross**. Bicycle riders started riding their bikes on motocross courses in the 1970s. The riders liked going over dirt jumps. They later began to build bikes for the new sport of BMX.

The sport has many fans today. Races for **amateurs** are popular worldwide. Riders of almost all ages compete. The best BMX racers are paid **professionals**.

EQUIPMENT

BMX racing bikes have small and lightweight frames. They have wide "knobby" tires with deep **tread**. The bumps and grooves of the tread give the tires a good grip on dirt and mud.

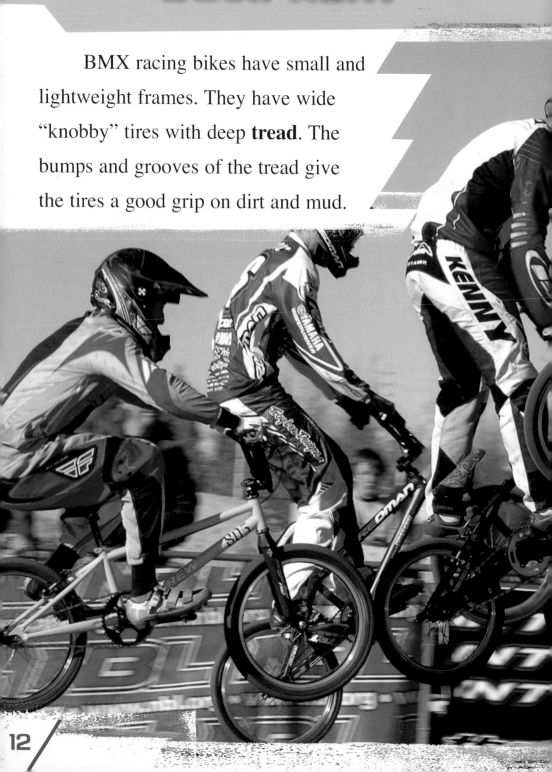

BMX bikes have just one gear. The bikes are tough and **durable**. They have to withstand a lot of hard riding.

Riders also need safety gear. Crashes can be dangerous. Riders are required to wear helmets. Many riders also wear a face shield or goggles to protect their face. Long sleeves, pants, and gloves are also important for safe riding.

BMX races are fast and exciting. Riders begin in a starting gate. They race around a track with many twists and turns. Riders sail over jumps and skid around banked **berms**. Most amateur races are short. They're often just a single lap. Professional races may include several laps.

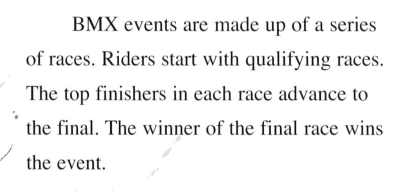

BMX events are made up of a series of races. Riders start with qualifying races. The top finishers in each race advance to the final. The winner of the final race wins the event.

STOP
ABSOLUTELY
NO RIDING ON
WET TRACK!

FAST FACT

The sport of
BMX freestyle, also
called bicycle stunt
riding, grew out of
BMX racing.

A single mistake can cost a BMX rider a win. The fast and exciting races feature sharp turns and big jumps. These are all reasons BMX racing is such a popular action sport.

GLOSSARY

amateur—someone who competes in a sport for fun rather than money

berm—a highly banked turn

durable—tough and long lasting

motocross—a sport in which riders drive dirt bikes around a small dirt course; motocross tracks include sharp turns and huge jumps.

professional—someone who is paid to compete in a sport

tread—the series of bumps and grooves on a tire that help it grip rough surfaces

TO LEARN MORE

AT THE LIBRARY

Blomquist, Christopher. *BMX in the X Games*.
New York: PowerKids Press, 2007.

Budd, E.S. *BMX Bicycles*. Chanhassen, Minn.:
Child's World, 2004.

Kaelberer, Angie Peterson. *BMX Racing*.
Mankato, Minn.: Capstone Press, 2006.

ON THE WEB

Learning more about bmx racing
is as easy as 1, 2, 3.

1. Go to www.factsurfer.com
2. Enter "bmx racing" into search box.
3. Click the "Surf" button and you will see a list
   of related web sites.

With factsurfer.com, finding more
information is just a click away.

INDEX

Bellwether wishes to thank the National Bicycle League (NBL) for their generous help with this book. For more information about NBL and BMX racing go to www.nbl.org.

The photographs in this book are reproduced through the courtesy of the National Bicycle League.